Pet H

by Nancy Lollo

PEARSON

Scott
Foresman

Editorial Offices: Glenview, Illinois • Parsippany, New Jersey • New York, New York
Sales Offices: Needham, Massachusetts • Duluth, Georgia • Glenview, Illinois
Coppell, Texas • Sacramento, California • Mesa, Arizona

Here are two pet helpers.
Do you know what they do?

dog trainer

This is a dog trainer.
A dog trainer trains dogs.

To train a dog means to teach.
He teaches dogs to jump up.
He trains dogs to sit.

puppy school

Take your puppy to a puppy school.
Your puppy will learn from a trainer.

This is a vet.
A vet is a doctor for animals.
Vets help all kinds of animals.

Vets help pets when they are sick.
Vets help pets to be healthy.

Trainers and vets are pet helpers.
How can they help a pet?